At the Feet of Jesus

At the Feet of Jesus

Daily Meditations

by Samantha Chambo

BEACON HILL PRESS
OF KANSAS CITY

Copyright © 2016 by Samantha Chambo
Beacon Hill Press of Kansas City
PO Box 419527
Kansas City, MO 64141
beaconhillbooks.com

978-0-8341-3604-5

All rights reserved. No part of this publication may be reproduced, stored in a retrieval system, or transmitted in any form or by any means—for example, electronic, photocopy, recording—without the prior written permission of the publisher. The only exception is brief quotations in printed reviews.

Cover Design: Merit Alcala
Interior Design: Sharon Page

Library of Congress Cataloging-in-Publication Data
Names: Chambo, Samantha, 1975- author.
Title: At the feet of Jesus : daily meditations / by Samantha Chambo.
Description: Kansas City, Missouri : Beacon Hill Press of Kansas City, 2016.
 | Includes bibliographical references.
Identifiers: LCCN 2016013280 | ISBN 9780834136045 (pbk.)
Subjects: LCSH: Jesus Christ—Biography—Meditations.
Classification: LCC BT306.43 .C43 2016 | DDC 242/.2—dc23 LC record available at https://lccn.loc.gov/2016013280

All Scripture quotations are taken from The *Holy Bible: New International Version*® (NIV®). Copyright © 1973, 1978, 1984, 2011 by Biblica, Inc.™ Used by permission of Zondervan. All rights reserved worldwide. www.zondervan.com.

The internet addresses, email addresses, and phone numbers in this book are accurate at the time of publication. They are provided as a resource. Beacon Hill Press of Kansas City does not endorse them or vouch for their content or permanence.

~ Contents

Preface	7
Day 1: Resist a Little Longer	8
Day 2: In the Power of the Holy Spirit	10
Day 3: Even the Demons Believe	12
Day 4: Deeper and to the Other Side	14
Day 5: I Am Willing	16
Day 6: The Old Is Better	18
Day 7: Persecution's Good	20
Day 8: Building on the Rock	22
Day 9: Help!	24
Day 10: True Wisdom	26
Day 11: Alabaster Box Attitude	28
Day 12: Open Eyes and Ears	30
Day 13: Who Is This Man?	32
Day 14: The Master's Touch	34
Day 15: A Suitable Jesus	36
Day 16: Saving Your Life	38
Day 17: The Power of Prayer	40
Day 18: No Looking Back	42
Day 19: The Joy of Jesus	44
Day 20: Hold the Fort!	46
Day 21: At the Feet of Jesus	48
Day 22: The Light in You	50
Day 23: Watchfulness	52
Day 24: Kingdom Judgment	54
Day 25: Finishing Well	56

Day 26: My Father's House	58
Day 27: Eternal Dwellings	60
Day 28: Be Ready	62
Day 29: Praying Right	64
Day 30: Finding Jesus above the Crowds	66
Day 31: The Authority of Jesus	68
Day 32: Stand Firm	70
Day 33: Like Wheat	72
Day 34: Pray against Temptation	74
Day 35: The Hour That Darkness Reigns	76
Day 36: A Sign of Some Sort	78
Day 37: The Wrath of God	80
Day 38: Entrusting Your Spirit	82
Day 39: Remember	84
Day 40: Burning Hearts	86
Day 41: Joy and Amazement	88
Day 42: A Cause for Great Joy	90

◈ Preface

This little devotional is the result of my own personal time with God. I read through traditional Lenten scriptures and was blessed by their wonder.

I realized that the suffering of Christ did not start on the road to Calvary. It started way before that, when he had to endure severe mental and emotional and physical distress in the wilderness where he was tempted for days; when he was rejected by his own people in Nazareth; when he was confronted with the hardness of heart present in those who were supposed to be spiritual leaders of Israel.

I also saw Jesus taking on the suffering of those he ministered to; I observed his compassion and empathy, his tears with those who mourned, and his desperation for the people he loved so much to accept the truth. My experience made me realize one thing: Jesus really understands all we encounter because he endured it all. This truth has been a source of great comfort to me, and I pray that it will be the same for those who choose to pick up this devotional.

May the realization of Christ's solidarity with us help us to show greater solidarity with those for whom he chose to die.

Day 1

Resist a Little Longer

Scripture Reading: Luke 4:1–13

Jesus, full of the Holy Spirit, left the Jordan and was led by the Holy Spirit into the wilderness, where for forty days he was tempted by the devil. He ate nothing during those days, and at the end of them he was hungry. (Luke 4:1–3)

Devotional Reflection

Jesus was tempted for forty days! I always read this passage thinking he only had to endure the three temptations mentioned in detail. However, the Holy Spirit has brought to my attention that Jesus was actually tempted for forty days and that the three temptations we read about are only the culmination of all he had to endure.

He was alone, hungry, and tired. This was forty days of severe mental, emotional, physical, and spiritual testing. Yet he did not relent or give up. He endured all that he needed to until the devil had to admit defeat and leave him for a season.

To me this speaks to endurance and perseverance in temptation. Satan will always hammer on the same spot, until we are left drained and ready to give up. But here we see our Savior as the perfect example of perseverance under temptation.

◈ Day 2

This perseverance is only possible for those who are "full of the Holy Spirit" (Luke 4:1). Even Jesus, the Son of God, had to be full of the Spirit before he could brave such severe testing. Apart from the Spirit we will fall.

Sometimes we just need to resist the devil a little longer, and he will flee from us.

Prayer

Lord, we know that you are faithful and that you will strengthen and protect us from the evil one. Please direct our hearts into God's love and Christ's perseverance. Amen. (2 Thessalonians 3:3, 5)

Meditation

1. What situations in your life are currently requiring perseverance?

2. What is God challenging you to do?

In the Power of the Holy Spirit

ಌ Day 3

Scripture Reading: Luke 4:14–30

Jesus returned to Galilee in the power of the Spirit, and news about him spread through the whole countryside. (Luke 4:14)

Devotional Reflection

Jesus was still filled with the power of the Holy Spirit when he returned to Nazareth to minister to his own people. Yet this did not guarantee his success. Jesus was rejected by his own people in spite of the obvious power of the Holy Spirit that was in and over him. They talked about him, and some even praised him, but Jesus knew what was really in their hearts.

It is the common expectation that the presence of the power of the Holy Spirit in our lives will ensure success for any endeavor we may be led by the Holy Spirit to undertake. However, we see from this example from the life of Jesus that people will reject even the power of the Holy Spirit if it threatens their comfort zones.

The natural result is to start doubting whether the Holy Spirit is really with us; we start questioning whether we are doing the right thing. Don't doubt. Jesus was not surprised at their reactions. He offered them the greatest gift from heaven, the salvation of their souls. They were blinded by what

Even the Demons Believe

they thought they knew about him. They missed the blessing as Jesus went on his way to offer it to those who would desperately grab on to it.

Not only did his people reject him; they also tried to kill him, which was no surprise to Jesus. He just slipped away to minister to those who would receive it. Persecution for the sake of righteousness is a given for those filled with the power of the Spirit. Let us not lose faith when persecution happens. We must remember that the blessed presence of God's Spirit is our companionship, our strength, and our victory.

Prayer

Father, you said that we are blessed when we are persecuted because of righteousness because the kingdom of heaven belongs to us. Help us to keep this in mind as we persevere in the power of your Holy Spirit. Amen. (Matthew 5:10)

Meditation

1. How has your commitment to God's call on your life affected your relationships?

❧ Day 4

2. What is God challenging you to do?

Scripture Reading: Luke 4:31–44

You believe that there is one God. Good! Even the demons believe that—and shudder. (James 2:19)

Devotional Reflection

What is extraordinary about our faith? How is it different from that of the demons? In this scripture, we see two occasions where Jesus rebuked demons, and they recognized him as the Messiah and submitted to his authority.

James chapter 2 teaches that it is our actions that make the difference. It is how we live our lives. Professing belief in the lordship of Jesus Christ is just lip service if our daily lives do not reflect our convictions.

Interestingly enough, Jesus rejected the testimony of the demons. He rebuked them to be quiet instead of proclaiming his identity to the very people he wanted to bring to faith. Jesus did not want to take the shortcut to get people to believe in him; he was

Deeper and to the Other Side

going to reveal his identify to them over a period of time, and those who would choose to believe in him would do so because they had a personal encounter with him.

Their belief would be more than just agreement due to a testimony; it would be confidence and trust based on personal acquaintance, and this would result in transformed lives.

We need to trust God with our very lives, acknowledging not just that he exists but also that he is a personal God who is able to save us. We can trust his judgment and timing in every aspect of our lives.

Prayer

Heavenly Father, please fill us with all joy and peace as we trust you so that we may overflow with hope by the power of the Holy Spirit. Amen. (Romans 15:13)

Meditation

1. How does your lifestyle reveal your trust in God?

Day 5

2. What is God challenging you to do?

I Am Willing

Scripture Reading: Luke 5:1–11

He said, "Throw your net on the right side of the boat and you will find some." When they did, they were unable to haul the net in because of the large number of fish. (John 21:6)

Devotional Reflection

The call to follow Jesus will always take us deeper than we ever planned to go and challenge us to do the opposite of what we would normally do.

Jesus's command to take their boats deeper and to throw their nets on the other side was just a foreshadowing of what discipleship would require from these simple fishermen in the future.

However, the great catch they got on this day could not compare to the great harvest they would reap once they became fishers of men. The church today is still a part of the catch for those faithful people who left everything behind to follow Jesus.

As disciples of Christ, we should be willing to go as deep as he commands and to do whatever he commands, even if we don't understand or agree. This way, we will experience the abundance that is a result of single-minded obedience.

➴ Day 6

Prayer

Holy Father, help us to trust in you with all our hearts and not to lean on our own understanding. Help us to submit to you in all our ways because we know that it is only you who makes our paths straight. Amen. (Proverbs 3:5–6)

Meditation

1. In which ways is God challenging you to get out of your comfort zone?

2. How will you respond?

The Old Is Better 🌿

Scripture Reading: Luke 5:12–26

Jesus reached out his hand and touched the man. "I am willing," he said. "Be clean!" And immediately the leprosy left him. (Luke 5:13)

Devotional Reflection

Jesus not only has the power to heal and restore us (Luke 5:17), but he is also willing. I have been on a journey of healing and restoration for some years now, and many times I got impatient with God. I wondered if he really wanted to heal me; maybe it was God's will that I be in this condition?

However, today's scripture is an encouragement to me. He is willing to heal me. That is why he came. Sometimes we have wrong beliefs about God. We are so aware of our sins and shortcomings that we always expect to be punished in some way.

Punishment for sin is not what the Bible teaches, though. Jesus Christ took our punishment on himself, and by his suffering, we are healed (Isaiah 53:4–5). God wants me to be whole in every aspect of my life—spiritually, mentally, emotionally, and physically.

God's will for our lives can only be good. We can surrender to him without reserve because he is willing.

Day 7

Prayer

Heal me, oh Lord, and I shall be healed; save me, and I shall be saved: for thou art my praise. Amen. (Jeremiah 17:14)

Meditation

1. In what areas of your life do you need healing and restoration?

2. What is God challenging you to do?

Persecution's Good

Scripture Reading: Luke 5:27–39

See, I am doing a new thing! Now it springs up; do you not perceive it? I am making a way in the wilderness and streams in the wasteland. (Isaiah 43:19)

Devotional Reflection

Jesus came to do a new thing. He called tax collectors to be his followers, he sat and ate with sinners, and his disciples did not fast. He did everything contrary to Pharisaic Judaism, which frustrated the Pharisees.

Jesus then used the analogy of the old and new garments and old and new wineskins to explain the newness of the kingdom. Jesus came to offer them a new and better way to stand in relation to God; however, they chose to hold on to the old ways. They preferred the old wineskins.

Jesus wants to move us forward to greater and better and higher things in him all the time. However, so many times we cling to the old, to the past, to the familiar, and in the process, we miss out on the greatest blessings of all.

May God help us not to resist the working of his Holy Spirit in our lives but, rather, to embrace it.

Day 8

Prayer

Oh Lord, open our eyes and turn us from darkness to light and from the power of Satan to God so that we may receive forgiveness of sins and a place among those who are sanctified by faith in thee. Amen. (Acts 26:18)

Meditation

1. Are there areas in your life where God is trying to make changes but you are resisting?

2. What is God challenging you to do today?

Building on the Rock

Scripture Reading: Luke 6:1–26

The Pharisees and the teachers of the law were looking for a reason to accuse Jesus, so they watched him closely to see if he would heal on the Sabbath. (Luke 6:7)

Devotional Reflection

The persecution of Jesus started long before the actual event of the cross. It followed him in the form of religious leaders every day of his life. In this scripture, Jesus and his disciples were just walking through a field. But the enemy was there, looking for an opportunity to accuse Jesus.

This did not surprise Jesus; in fact, he expected it. It did hurt and make him angry because their hearts were so hardened. In verses 17–26, Jesus explains that hardship and difficulty and persecution are a given for those whose hearts are committed to seeking the kingdom of God. This exact difficulty will lead to great blessings in the lives of these people.

Jesus did not face the challenges of his mission in his own power. He spent the whole of the previous night in prayer, primarily for guidance to choose his disciples, but I am sure he also prayed for all the challenges he knew he would face the following day.

Sometimes the calling to live a totally surrendered life will be painful and difficult. It might require us

Day 9

to defend the kingdom, to face excommunication from popular crowds or even from our loved ones. This is common to the narrow way. Let us keep our eyes on Jesus at all times.

Prayer

Jesus, we know that a servant is not greater than his master. If they persecuted you, they will also persecute us. Help us to remain faithful and walk in obedience in spite of adversity. Amen. (John 15:20)

Meditation

1. Are you experiencing any form of persecution as a result of your commitment to Christ?

2. What is God challenging you to do today?

Help!

Scripture Reading: Luke 6:27–49

But the one who hears my words and does not put them into practice is like a man who built a house on the ground without a foundation. The moment the torrent struck that house, it collapsed and its destruction was complete. (Luke 6:49)

Devotional Reflection

Jesus taught the secret of true security. It lies in listening and doing what he commands. His commands can be difficult, but the results of obeying them are blessings. Jesus explained what true surrender means. It means treating others as we want to be treated; it means leaving judging up to God; it means loving our enemies and bearing good fruit.

The wise person puts the teachings of Jesus into practice. This is the real sign of repentance—a transformed life. It is a life that conforms to the Word because of an inner attitude of love and surrender to Christ as Savior.

Torrents will come in our lives; we just need to make sure our lives are built on the Rock that is Jesus Christ.

Day 10

Prayer

Father, please help us to not merely listen to the Word, and so deceive ourselves. Help us to do what it says. Help us to look intently into your law that brings freedom so that we can be blessed in what we do. Amen. (James 1:22–25)

Meditation

1. What are the things and conditions you normally look to for security?

2. What is God challenging you to do today?

True Wisdom

Scripture Reading: Luke 7:1–17

They were all filled with awe and praised God. "A great prophet has appeared among us," they said. "God has come to help his people." (Luke 7:16)

Devotional Reflection

I found it interesting to compare the two accounts of healing in this chapter. First, we see a situation where Jesus is literally begged to heal a young servant. In contrast, the widow did not even ask; Jesus simply chose to raise her son from the dead. Emphasis is placed on the faith of the centurion, while none was required of the widow. However, in both situations, we see Jesus ready to fulfill his mission to bring God's grace to humans.

The crowds were correct when they said, "God has come to help his people," even though they did not understand what they were saying. Their understanding was limited to what they could see. Even greater than these miracles would be the spiritual life Jesus would provide to all who would receive it by faith.

It is wonderful to know that Christ wants to heal and restore us. Our wholeness does not depend on the amount of faith we have. It depends on his love for us. Just as he was filled with compassion for the

~ Day 11

widow, so he has compassion on every soul that labors under a burden of sin.

Prayer

Father, thank you that you show no partiality. Thank you that you are not willing that any should die but that everyone should have abundant life in you. Amen. (Acts 10:34)

Meditation

1. In what areas of your life do you need help today?

2. What is God challenging you to do?

Alabaster Box Attitude

Day 12

Scripture Reading: Luke 7:18–35

But wisdom is proved right by all her children. (Luke 7:35)

Devotional Reflection

Jesus and John the Baptist came to preach the message of repentance in two very different ways, yet the Pharisees rejected both. It did not matter how the message was packaged; they were not willing to repent, and therefore, they rejected it.

Jesus compared them to children who refused to respond when invited by other children (John and Jesus) to play. Jesus then goes on to say that wisdom will be proved right by her children. I initially thought this meant that Jesus would rise up and prove the truth of the gospel. However, after studying it a bit more, I realized that the wisdom of the gospel is proven by *us*.

We are the children of the gospel; we gladly accepted the message and repented of our sins. Now it is our lives, our practices, that will prove to those who rejected it that it was the truth from God. We do this by living authentic lives that proclaim the manifestation of the gospel on earth.

Open Eyes and Ears

Prayer

Father, help our light shine so brightly before people that they will see our good works and glorify our Father in heaven. Amen. (Matthew 5:16)

Meditation

1. In which ways does your life reflect the wisdom of the gospel?

2. What is God challenging you to do today?

❧ Day 13

Scripture Reading: Luke 7:36–50

Therefore, I tell you, her many sins have been forgiven—as her great love has shown. But whoever has been forgiven little loves little. (Luke 7:47)

Devotional Reflection

This event highlights two attitudes—that of Simon and that of the sinful woman. Simon was self-righteous, self-sufficient, and critical of Jesus. He invited Jesus in order to scrutinize and figure him out. He had no need of a Savior. It is clear from the events that Simon did nothing extra to show appreciation for Jesus. He did not call the servant to wash Jesus's feet, and he did not greet him with a kiss or even put some olive oil on his head, as some people were accustomed to doing for a special guest.

The sinful woman, on the other hand, came in brokenness, desperation, surrender, and overwhelming love to Jesus. She knew she had nothing in herself that could save her and that Jesus was her only hope. Her actions proved her attitude. She threw herself at his feet, wept over him, kissed him, and anointed him with precious oil. It seems as if this sinful woman has received a knowledge that was kept from the religious leader: She knew in her heart who Jesus was. That is why she did not lose the opportunity to throw herself at his mercy. She also knew who *she* was—thus, her desperation.

Who Is This Man?

We should strive to live in this attitude of absolute love and adoration—an attitude of total dependence and surrender. We must acknowledge every day that we are hopeless to save ourselves; our sufficiency comes from Jesus. Only then will we be able to live in the assurance that this sinful woman had when she left the presence of Jesus. She knew she was forgiven.

Prayer

Father, help us to have the same mindset of Christ Jesus. He made himself nothing, became a servant, humbled himself, and was obedient even to death on a cross. Amen. (Philippians 2:5–11)

Meditation

1. Is your attitude like that of Simon or of the sinful woman?

2. What is God challenging you to do today?

Day 14

Scripture Reading: Luke 8:1–18

Therefore consider carefully how you listen. Whoever has will be given more; whoever does not have, even what they think they have will be taken from them. (Luke 8:18)

Devotional Reflection

In a civilized society soaked with religion, people claim to hear God speaking all around us. However, merely hearing the Word of God is not enough; there is a specific requirement about how we hear if we are going to retain, or even benefit from, the Word.

In the parable of the sower, it is obvious that the farmer sows generously and equally to all the ground; however, it is also clear that the various conditions of the ground are set before the sower even sows. Some come with hardened hearts, some come frivolously, and some come with their attention occupied by so many things around them. The result is that the Word cannot take permanent root in their hearts.

The watermark that reveals the quality of the listener is the fruit or, as mentioned in verse 16, the light that emanates from those who have been changed by the Word. We can determine what type of listeners we ourselves are by the light we provide to those around us (or the lack thereof). Another way to look at it is found in verse 17; the light of God will disclose the hidden secrets of our hearts, and then there will be no question.

We must eagerly cherish the Word of God as precious to our very lives because it can be taken away from us. The Word is life to our very souls; it is the rough material that will build our faith. We must listen eagerly and with an insatiable hunger; then we will be satisfied, and we will receive even more from God.

Prayer

Father, thank you for your words that are life to our souls. Help us to delight in your law and to meditate on it day and night. Then we will be fruitful, like a tree planted by streams of water, and yield our fruit in season. Then our leaves will not wither, and all our endeavors will prosper. Amen. (Psalm 1:2–3)

Meditation

1. If you judge by the fruit that is apparent in your life, would you classify yourself as a good listener or not?

Day 15

2. What is God challenging you to do today?

Scripture Reading: Luke 8:22-39

In fear and amazement they asked one another, "Who is this?" (Luke 8:25b)

Devotional Reflection

The question about who Jesus is, is of the utmost importance. A. W. Tozer said, "No religion has ever been greater than its idea of God."[1] Our concept of Jesus's identity has direct implications on the lives we will live as Christians.

The disciples obviously had not come to the full realization of who Jesus was at this point of the story, and they reacted with surprise and amazement when he calmed the storm. Jesus rebuked them for their lack of sufficient faith in him. Their fear was proof of their lack of knowledge.

The second portion of this scripture also puts the spotlight on Jesus's identity. In this scenario he was confronted by a demon-possessed man. The demon

1. A. W. Tozer, *The Knowledge of the Holy: The Attributes of God: Their Meaning in the Christian Life* (New York: Harper and Row, 1961), 9.

A Suitable Jesus

immediately recognized him as the Son of God and begged Jesus to spare them. The man was faced with the person of Jesus when he was delivered from a legion of demons, and his response was to beg Jesus
to allow him to go with Jesus. The people of the Gerasenes who witnessed the miracle responded to the revelation of Jesus in fear and begged him to leave their region.

We can determine what we think of Jesus by looking at our own response to his presence and to circumstances we face on a daily basis. Do we panic and become desperate when life gets a bit rough? Do we recoil in fear at the revelation of God in our lives, or do we rush after him and beg him to allow us to follow him?

Prayer

Jesus, we know that you are the Messiah, the Son of the living God. Help us to live our daily lives in the victory and liberation that this truth commands. Amen. (Matthew 16:16)

Meditation

1. How do you respond today to the revelation of Jesus in your life?

Day 16

2. What is God challenging you to do today?

Scripture Reading: Luke 8:40–56

But Jesus said, "Someone touched me; I know that power has gone out from me." (Luke 8:46)

Devotional Reflection

This scripture introduces two very different ladies who both experience the life-changing effect of the Master's touch. One was a privileged child of a synagogue leader and the other a poor, desperate woman who had been suffering from bleeding for twelve years.

We see some common aspects in both of these stories. First, we see that the touch was intentional. In the story of the sick lady, the intent came from her side. She was so desperate that she was willing to do anything just for an opportunity to touch Jesus. In the story of the little girl, the intent came from Jesus. He deliberately went to her house, knowing she had died, reached out and pulled her by the hand, and commanded her to live again.

Another thing we see in both stories is the exceedingly great power of the touch of Jesus. This power healed an incurable disease that had been plaguing the woman for twelve years, and the little girl was powerfully raised from the dead.

We also see the wonderful change that Jesus's touch brought about for these two ladies. For the older lady, it meant the end of twelve years of suffering and pain; it meant a life of wholeness and restoration. For the little girl, it meant a second chance at life; she was literally raised from the dead.

We need to have the same intent and desperation for a touch from God. We must be like Jacob, who said to the angel of the Lord, "I will not let you go unless you bless me" (Genesis 32:26). While we do this, we can rest assured in the knowledge that Jesus has already reached out to us and continues to pursue us with great intent.

Prayer

Father, I know your arm is not too short to save me, and your ear is not too dull to hear me. Thank you for your touch in my life. Amen. (Isaiah 59:1)

Meditation

1. Think of the areas in your life where you need a touch from Jesus.

Day 17

2. What is God challenging you to do today?

Scripture Reading: Luke 9:1–20

"But what about you?" he asked. "Who do you say I am?" (Luke 9:20)

Devotional Reflection

This is another occasion when we find people grappling with the identity of Jesus. Jesus sent out the disciples to preach the good news about the kingdom, and the recipients of the message reacted differently. They found themselves speculating about the identity of Jesus.

Herod the tetrarch hoped that Jesus was John the Baptist come back from the dead. This was because Herod had beheaded John against his better judgment (Matthew 14:1–12), and he had some unresolved issues with John, so he really wanted to see Jesus. The crowds saw Jesus as the source of miracles and healing. They saw him as their source for bread, which was why they followed him.

The Power of Prayer

It is interesting that this question was important to Jesus. He asked Peter what people thought of him. He was interested to know whether they'd gotten the message right. They obviously missed it. But Peter did not. He made a bold confession that Jesus was the Christ.

The question we are faced with is this: *Who do you say I am?* Who is Jesus to me?

Why am I seeking him? Is it because I have unresolved issues, or because I see him as the source of all my needs, or is it because of who he is—the Christ, the Son of the living God?

Prayer

Jesus, we have come to believe and know that you are the holy One of God. Help us to live our daily lives in the wonder of this great truth. Amen. (John 6:69)

Meditation

1. Why are you seeking Jesus today?

Day 18

2. What is God challenging you to do today?

No Looking Back

Scripture Reading: Luke 9:21–27

For whoever wants to save their life will lose it, but whoever loses their life for me will save it. (Luke 9:24)

Devotional Reflection

Just as the suffering and death of Jesus was a divine necessity if we are to be saved, so our death to self is needed if we are going to be truly alive. We do not have a choice as to whether we will relinquish our worldly concepts of the good life; we must, in order to save our souls.

This dying to self involves a reorientation of our priorities, a willingness to suffer for the advancement of the gospel, and a decision to follow Jesus, living according to the example he has set for us.

This radical devotion to Jesus is in direct contrast to the world, and it will require boldness and courage to live faithfully to Jesus and to his Word. We have to be willing to stand out as fanatics in the eyes of modern humans. However, we have this promise: Christ will acknowledge us before his Father in heaven if we persevere.

Day 19

Prayer

Father, help us not be ashamed of the gospel because it is the power of God that brings salvation to everyone who believes. Amen. (Romans 1:16)

Meditation

1. Are there areas remaining in your life where you need to die to self?

2. What is God challenging you to do today?

The Joy of Jesus

Scripture Reading: Luke 9:28–36

As he was praying, the appearance of his face changed, and his clothes became as bright as a flash of lightning. (Luke 9:29)

Devotional Reflection

Prayer not only changes situations and problems; it also changes *us*. Jesus went up on the mountain to pray, and as he was praying, his appearance became radiant and glorious. It reminds us of the account in Exodus when Moses spent time on the mountain in fellowship with God, and his face shone so brightly that, when he came down, he had to cover it with a veil.

Another instance when prayer changed Jesus was in the garden of Gethsemane. He went into the garden in anxiety and turmoil and left in a steady determination to accomplish the salvation of humanity. If prayer could change the Savior, then I am sure it can change us.

Prayer

Holy Father, thank you for removing the veil of ignorance from our faces. Thank you that we can contemplate your glory. Thank you that we are being transformed into your image with ever-increasing glory, which comes from you.

Day 20

Help us to always seek your face. Amen. (2 Corinthians 3:18)

Meditation

1. Think of special times you have spent in prayer and how it has changed you.

2. What is God challenging you to do today?

Hold the Fort!

Scripture Reading: Luke 9:37–62

Jesus replied, "No one who puts a hand to the plow and looks back is fit for service in the kingdom of God." (Luke 9:62)

Devotional Reflection

One of the most difficult aspects of following Jesus pertains to our families. Sometimes we have to follow Jesus in spite of their counsel. Sometimes we have to leave them behind, and this hurts. Other times God directs us to address their sins, and this could cause estrangement from people we love.

At such times, the road becomes really narrow, and looking back becomes a real temptation. In 1 Kings 19:20, Elijah allowed Elisha to go back and greet his family. But this is not allowed when we choose to follow Jesus. "The dead [must] bury their own dead" (Luke 9:60).

The temptation to look back is greater when it is the ones we love pulling at our heartstrings. However, in times like these, we have to follow the example of Jesus. "Jesus resolutely set out for Jerusalem" (Luke 9:51b).

Day 21

Prayer

Lord, please help us not to fix our eyes on what is seen but on what is unseen because what is seen is temporary, but what is unseen is eternal. Amen. (2 Corinthians 4:18)

Meditation

1. Does your relationship to your family hinder or encourage your devotion to God?

2. What is God challenging you to do today?

At the Feet of Jesus

Scripture Reading: Luke 10:1-24

At that time Jesus, full of joy through the Holy Spirit, said, "I praise you, Father, Lord of heaven and earth, because you have hidden these things from the wise and learned, and revealed them to little children. Yes, Father, for this is what you were pleased to do." (Luke 10:21)

Devotional Reflection

What brings joy to Jesus? In this scripture, we see that Jesus sent out seventy-two disciples to preach the gospel. They came back full of joy and excitement and reported great victory and freedom for those who accepted their message. They got it! They understood what the kingdom of God was all about.

Jesus, in his prayer of praise and thanksgiving to the Father, mentions that God has revealed the great secrets of heaven to the simple and the uneducated instead of all the learned, wise scribes and Pharisees. To those who, by faith, accepted the great truth that the kingdom of God was near and had arrived.

We can compare this to the frustration that Jesus expressed earlier when his disciples came back and showed little understanding of the kingdom principle. Jesus mentioned their lack of faith. God revealed even more to the intimate twelve, yet they

Day 22

fell short in their faith in comparison to this larger group.

Jesus rejoices when we accept the revelation of the kingdom by faith and are able to go out and act upon it in faith.

Prayer

Father, send us your light and your truth and let them guide us; let them bring us to your holy mountain, to the place where you dwell. Amen. (Psalm 43:3)

Meditation

1. How open are you to God's revelation of his truth in your life?

2. What is God challenging you to do today?

The Light in You

❧ Day 23

Scripture Reading: Luke 10:25–37

"Which of these three do you think was a neighbor to the man who fell into the hands of robbers?"

The expert in the law replied, "The one who had mercy on him."

Jesus told him, "Go and do likewise." (Luke 10:36–37)

Devotional Reflection

The condition of the victim in this parable may be seen in a spiritual light. It could be a believer who has been so bruised and battered by Satan that their faith is hanging on by a thread. It could be a believer on the verge of backsliding, ready to turn their back on God forever.

The Jewish leaders who passed by can be compared to fellow believers—those of the house of faith who are so busy with their own lives that they have no time to help a drowning brother or sister. Those who look down on weak believers and condemn them for their failures and indiscretions. Those who kick their brothers and sisters while they are taking their last spiritual breaths.

Satan is out like a roaring lion, and he is devouring the believers. We need to remember that our struggle is not against flesh and blood but against the evil spirits of this age. That is why we must put

Watchfulness

on the full armor of God so that we may be able to stand and pull up our comrades who have fallen in battle.

Can we administer the wine and oil of the Word and the Spirit to those who are bleeding to death? Can we drag them to safety for the sake of the cross?

Prayer

Father, we put on the full armor of God today. Help us pray in the Spirit on all occasions with all kinds of prayers and requests. Help us to keep this in mind, to be alert, and always keep on praying for all of the Lord's people. Amen. (Ephesians 6:13–18)

Meditation

1. Are there believers in your life whom you know have fallen away or are falling away at this time?

2. What is God challenging you to do today?

Day 24

Scripture Reading: Luke 10:38–42

"Martha, Martha," the Lord answered, "you are worried and upset about many things, but few things are needed—or indeed only one. Mary has chosen what is better, and it will not be taken away from her." Luke 10:41–42

Devotional Reflection

Jesus told Martha that she was worried about many things—in other words, that she needed to relax. What was she worried about? Did she worry about whether her guests were comfortable, whether there was enough food, whether everyone was enjoying themselves? Or maybe she was worried about her sister. Maybe she worried that Mary was not behaving in a proper way or that she was not showing any consideration to her older sister? Jesus could see that she was overburdened, and he felt compassion for her. We see his understanding of her urgency when he addressed her by repeating her name twice.

Mary chose to sit at the feet of Jesus. What a blessed place. It is a place where we can forget about all our worries and shortcomings and just listen. Mary was able to soak up the words of Jesus and store them in her heart. She was able to feast her eyes on his glorious face. She chose the best way.

Kingdom Judgment

Consciously choosing to forget about all that troubles us and just sit at the feet of Jesus is difficult. Many times we find our minds going in all directions even while we try to get some devotional time in. Sitting at the feet of Jesus means shutting everything out and listening with your heart. It means everything and all people fade into the background so Jesus can become the focus of our souls.

Prayer

Father, one thing we ask of you and this only we seek, that we may dwell in your house all the days of our lives, to gaze on thy beauty and to seek you in your holy temple. Amen. (Psalm 27:4)

Meditation

1. What are the things that worry you most at this moment?

2. What is God challenging you to do today?

Day 25

Scripture Reading: Luke 11

See to it, then, that the light within you is not darkness.
(Luke 11:35)

Devotional Reflection

It is so easy to be deceived. To labor for the Lord and to believe you are doing his will while you are slowly drifting away from him.

This was the case with the scribes and Pharisees. They were zealous for the things of God, but they focused so much on the outside that they neglected their inner persons. They were so caught up in obeying the law that they missed the very presence of the Messiah they had been waiting for all this time.

This is a very sad situation. Jesus confronted them about their wrong attitudes and their spiritual blindness. However, instead of falling at his feet in repentance, they began plotting against him. This is the reason he said the people of Nineveh would testify against them. Nineveh was so wicked that God planned to destroy it; however, the people repented when Jonah confronted them with their sins and told them to repent. They believed and obeyed.

Finishing Well

Prayer

Father, help us to believe and obey the words you speak to us. Help us to respond like Nineveh when we are confronted with our sin so that we may find grace and mercy from you. Amen. (Luke 11:28)

Meditation

1. What external things do you hold on to so tightly that you are prevented from listening to God?

2. What is God challenging you to do today?

❦ Day 26

Scripture Reading: Luke 12

Be dressed and ready for service and keep your lamps burning. (Luke 12:35)

Devotional Reflection

The kingdom of God is here. It has arrived with the coming of Jesus Christ as a human being, and we chose to be part of the kingdom when we accepted Christ as our Lord and Savior.

However, while we wait for the glorious appearance of Jesus, life is happening. There are so many difficulties, things to worry about, things we want to achieve and acquire, people we want to win over. There are also so many distractions by means of the media and social networks. It is so easy to get swallowed up in the things of this world and forget that we are supposed to be from a different kingdom.

Jesus made it clear that he wants us to live in this world but always keep in mind that we are citizens of a heavenly kingdom. We must be watchful in prayer so that we don't lose our focus on the purposes of God. We are stewards of the kingdom, and we will be judged according to how we manifest it in this world.

The Bible says that we purify ourselves if we live in the hope of the return of Christ. We cannot afford

My Father's House

to get caught up with the things that occupy the lives of unbelievers. Jesus is coming back soon, and we want to be ready. That is why we must live our lives detached from worldly passions.

Prayer

Father, we know how to interpret the appearance of the earth and sky. Please help us also know how to interpret the present time. Help us live in a state of readiness for your return. Amen. (Luke 12:56)

Meditation

1. How are you making sure that you stay alert and watchful in your spiritual life?

2. What is God challenging you to do?

Day 27

Scripture Reading: Luke 13

But unless you repent, you too will all perish. (Luke 13:3)

Devotional Reflection

There is a mindset amongst Christians that judgment and the execution of that judgment is an Old Testament thing. We believe that we live in a dispensation of grace and can therefore experience the joys of the kingdom without worrying about judgment.

The harsh words of judgment in Luke 13 come as a surprise. Jesus said a lot about judgment and warned the people to repent because they might find themselves out of the kingdom where there will be weeping and gnashing of teeth (Luke 13:27).

He speaks extensively about the importance of bearing the fruits of repentance, which signifies living a life that is in line with our confession of faith; otherwise we might find ourselves cut off (Luke 13:1–7). We also see that Jesus had great sorrow for his people who refused to accept his words because he loved them and did not want them to be cut off (Luke 13:34–35).

God's judgment is as real in the New Testament as it is in the Old Testament. However, we must focus on

Eternal Dwellings

bearing the fruits of the kingdom (Galatians 5:22), which will ensure our reception "at the feast in the kingdom of God" (Luke 13:29).

Prayer

Father, since we have been raised with Christ, help us set our hearts on things above, where Christ is seated at the right hand of God. Help us set our minds on things above, not on earthly things. For we died, and our lives are now hidden with Christ in God. When Christ, who is our life, appears, then we also will appear with him in glory. Amen. (Colossians 3:1–4)

Meditation

1. Is your life bearing the fruits of the kingdom of Christ?

2. What is God challenging you to do today?

Day 28

Be Ready

Scripture Reading: Luke 14

For if you lay the foundation and are not able to finish it, everyone who sees it will ridicule you. (Luke 14:29)

Devotional Reflection

It is important to understand the full implication of a decision to follow Jesus. It requires that the followers give up everything and put Jesus above everything—even our closest family relationships, even our own lives.

In the parable of the banquet, we see people making excuses when they are invited. They put family relationships, their means of living, and the cares of their lives above the invitation to the great banquet. Jesus is addressing those who refuse to follow him for the same reasons. Because of their out-of-order priorities, they lose their opportunity to enter the kingdom of God.

However, I wonder if these individuals might not have been better off than those who eagerly followed Jesus without counting the cost and then found themselves incapable of making the sacrifices needed. These are the people who get ridiculed because they started on the journey of faith and gave up on the way. Those who give up are like tasteless salt—useless.

Day 29

Praying Right

Prayer

Father, please help us to forget what is behind and strain toward what is ahead. Help us to press on toward the goal to win the prize for which God has called us heavenward in Christ Jesus. Amen. (Philippians 3:13–14)

Meditation

1. Have you taken the time to consider the cost of following Jesus?

2. What is God challenging you to do today?

Day 30

Scripture Reading: Luke 15

"My son," the father said, "you are always with me, and everything I have is yours." (Luke 15:31)

Devotional Reflection

It seems that it is always the problem children who get the most attention. Parents are caught up in trying to save and rehabilitate these prodigals, while the faithful children are sometimes left to feel invisible.

Feeling invisible is not always a reflection of reality, though. This scripture is clear that the father was aware of his oldest son; he knew that his son was always with him. He also determined that everything that he owned belonged to this faithful son. He had such peace with the condition of the oldest that he felt secure enough to receive the lost son with great love.

The fact is that the shepherd would go after any of the sheep that got lost, and the lady would have searched just as eagerly for any of her other coins. Each one of these was valued just because they belonged to the owner. In the case of the sons, the father valued both sons on the simple basis that they were his children. However, he valued his oldest son because that son chose to remain faithful to

Finding Jesus above the Crowds

his father. His faithfulness made his reward even greater.

Prayer

Heavenly Father, help us to have patient endurance and keep your commands and remain faithful to you (Revelation 14:12). We know that you have called us into fellowship with your Son, Jesus Christ, and that you are faithful and will keep us firm to the end so that we will be blameless on the day of our Lord Jesus Christ. Amen. (1 Corinthians 1:8)

Meditation

1. Do you ever feel invisible in God's house?

2. In what ways is God giving you assurance today?

Day 31

The Authority of Jesus

Scripture Reading: Luke 16

I tell you, use worldly wealth to gain friends for yourselves, so that when it is gone, you will be welcomed in eternal dwellings. (Luke 16:9)

Devotional Reflection

It seems as if the church has lost its emphasis on the hereafter. A few decades ago people were very aware of the reality of our final destinations, and preachers preached about it often. However, these days, there is so much emphasis on having a good life here on earth that this vital part of our beliefs is getting neglected.

Jesus spoke about the hereafter often, and Luke 16 is another example. He exhorted his listeners to be careful how they used their possessions and how they treated people because all of it would have bearing on where they would spend eternity—heaven or hell.

Everything and every relationship we have the privilege of experiencing here on earth is a gift from God. We must be good stewards so God can trust us with even greater things. Not only that, but we will be assured of our place in heaven.

Day 32

Prayer

Jesus, we know you have gone to prepare a place for us so we can be where you are. Help us to live our lives in such a way that we are worthy to enter the joy of your eternal kingdom. Amen. (John 14:1–4)

Meditation

1. Are you living your life in such a way that you will be welcomed in heaven one day?

2. What is God challenging you to do today?

Stand Firm

Scripture Reading: Luke 17

For the Son of Man in his day will be like the lightning, which flashes and lights up the sky from one end to the other. (Luke 17:24)

Devotional Reflection

The second coming of Christ will be the most spectacular and awe-inspiring event history has ever seen. Jesus will not come quietly in a little town, as he did the first time. At his return, every eye will see him, and every knee will bow before him.

It is also going to be unexpected. Life will go on as usual until, suddenly, he appears in all his glory. That is why it is so important to be ready at all times. No one knows the day or the hour, only God. We have to make sure we continue to live by faith in God's Son, to live in humility and servanthood before God and people, and to live lives that bring glory and praise to God.

This also implies an urgency to proclaim the good news that the kingdom of God has come (Luke 17:21). We must labor to call people to faith in the Son of God; otherwise it will be like in the days of Noah, and we might just have to watch our loved ones being left behind.

Day 33

Prayer

Father, we pray that you strengthen our hearts so we will be blameless and holy in the presence of our God and Father when our Lord Jesus comes with all his holy ones. Amen. (1 Thessalonians 3:13)

Meditation

1. To what degree are you working to ensure that as many people as possible will be ready at the second coming of Jesus?

2. What is God challenging you to do?

Like Wheat

Scripture Reading: Luke 18

For all those who exalt themselves will be humbled, and those who humble themselves will be exalted. (Luke 18:14b)

Devotional Reflection

Prayer has always been a tricky issue to me. There were so many times when I wondered, *Am I doing it right? Are my prayers acceptable? Is God hearing me?* All my anxiety was unnecessary, of course. Praying is talking to God with a sincere heart, and God will always hear and respond to such a heart.

Luke 18 highlights some of the things God looks for in those who come to him in prayer. In the parable of the persistent widow, we see that he expects us to persevere in prayer, never to give up. We must continue to pray even when we don't see immediate results, and God will "bring about justice for his chosen ones, who cry out to him day and night" (Luke 18:7).

In the parable of the tax collector and also the incident with the children, it becomes clear that God expects us to come with a humble, repentant heart if we are to receive mercy. From the children we also learn the importance of childlike faith when we come in prayer. From the rich ruler we learn that our possessions can be a hindrance in our relation-

Day 34

ship with God if they are more important to us than our love for God. Lastly we see the bold desperation of the blind beggar. Nothing was going to stop him from receiving his miracle.

I think it is wonderful that God did not leave us in the dark concerning what he expects of us when we come to him in prayer. This reveals his heart of love and his desire to be even more intimate with us.

Prayer

We call on you, Lord, come quickly to us, and hear us when we call to you. May our prayers be set before you like incense; may the lifting up of our hands be like the evening sacrifice. Amen. (Psalm 141:1–2)

Meditation

1. Are you satisfied with your prayer life?

2. What is God challenging you to do today?

Pray against Temptation

Day 35

Scripture Reading: Luke 19

He wanted to see who Jesus was, but because he was short he could not see over the crowd. (Luke 19:3)

Devotional Reflection

I think we can all identify with Zacchaeus's dilemma. He had a strong desire to get to know Jesus, but there were just too many people crowding him out. In our lives it is not just people but things, situations, and the stress of life that can make it difficult to experience Jesus in our daily lives. Sometimes we just need to do what Zacchaeus did and try to rise above it all to get a glimpse of Jesus.

The story of the ten minas is about the final judgment: The basis on which we will be judged will be our response to Jesus. We will be deemed as good and faithful servants when we, like Zacchaeus, do all we can to draw closer to Jesus and repent of our sins and make amends where necessary.

However, we might find ourselves in the position of those who were driven out of the temple because they were so busy with earthly things that they missed Jesus. They were so busy with religious activities that they missed the Lord of all.

Jesus is the King of kings and the Lord of lords, and one day when he returns, it will all be revealed. We

The Hour That Darkness Reigns

must be sure we are not like the worshipers who ushered him into Jerusalem singing *Hosanna*, only to shout, "Crucify him!" a short while later.

Prayer

Father, our souls thirst for you, for the living God. When can we go and meet with God? (Psalm 42:2). You promised that we will never be thirsty again if we believe in you (John 6:35). Help us to seek you with our whole hearts. Amen.

Meditation

1. Do you have a consistent desire to find Jesus in every aspect of your daily life?

2. What is God challenging you to do today?

Day 36

Scripture Reading: Luke 20

Everyone who falls on that stone will be broken to pieces; anyone on whom it falls will be crushed. (Luke 20:18)

Devotional Reflection

Does Jesus have full authority in your life? Can he turn over tables and rebuke bad attitudes and beliefs as he sees fit? The religious leaders did not recognize the authority of Jesus. They saw him as an imposter who created confusion in the community, and their greatest aim was to get rid of him.

Jesus's authority does not depend on our response to him. We can accept him as Lord of our lives or reject him, as in the case of the religious leaders. This will not change the fact that he is the Son of God and that God has given him all authority in heaven and on earth. This means he will stand as judge over the responses of all those called to his kingdom.

The judgment meted out to those who reject Jesus will be devastating; they will be crushed, according to Luke. Why would it be this harsh? Because they should have known better. They were entrusted with the truth of Scripture, the priesthood, and prophecy, but they chose to create a religion suitable to themselves. This will result in their ultimate destruction.

A Sign of Some Sort

Recognizing the authority of Jesus means we allow ourselves to be shaped according to his pleasure. We will repent when needed and obey when commanded. It means Jesus has the final say on every aspect of our lives.

Prayer

Jesus, we know that all authority in heaven and on earth has been given to you. We proclaim you as Lord of our lives and submit to your sovereign will. Amen. (Matthew 28:18)

Meditation

1. Does Christ have full authority in your life?

2. What is God challenging you to do today?

Day 37

The Wrath of God

Scripture Reading: Luke 21

Stand firm, and you will win life. (Luke 21:19)

Devotional Reflection

We are living in the end times. All that Jesus has mentioned and predicted is happening right before our eyes. Even the church has surrendered to worldliness and tolerance of all that is wrong. The few who choose to hold on to the true gospel are the ones being persecuted.

Sometimes we can start to rationalize and come to the conclusion that a more tolerant, open religious attitude will take us further. However, we must not allow ourselves to be deceived; there is no easy way to live as a follower of Christ in this fallen world. Persecution and misunderstanding cannot be avoided when we express our faith and call people to repentance.

We must be vigilant and pray at all times. We cannot allow ourselves to be distracted by the passions, cares, and entertainment of this world (Luke 21:36). Even good things and good people might be tools in the hands of Satan to divert us from God's holy calling.

To stand firm means to take a stance of steady power and strength; it means to endure and to per-

Day 38

severe. It means to have a focused determination to reach our goal, which is the salvation of our souls. It implies difficulty but also victory.

Prayer

Father, help us to be faithful, even to the point of death, because we know that you promised to give us a victor's crown. Amen. (Revelation 2:10)

Meditation

1. What signs of the times mentioned by Jesus in this chapter are you aware of in society?

2. What circumstances require that you stand firm?

3. What is Christ challenging you to do today?

Entrusting Your Spirit

Scripture Reading: Luke 22:1–38

Satan has asked to sift all of you as wheat. (Luke 22:31)

Devotional Reflection

The cross was drawing near. Judas arranged to betray Jesus. They sat together to eat the Passover meal, and Jesus urgently began to prepare them for the events that were about to take place. Jesus had spoken about all of this before, but he knew his disciples did not get it—hence the urgency.

During supper, Jesus initiated what we now know as the Lord's Supper. He explained that it represents his broken body and his shed blood, that it was a symbol of the new covenant. But still they had no understanding. Instead they started to dispute about who should be the greatest in Jesus's kingdom.

During all of this discussion, Jesus mentioned that Satan had asked to sift them like wheat. More importantly, it would be the events that led up to the cross that would be the means of sifting. It would be their response to Jesus and his suffering and resurrection that would separate the wheat from the chaff.

The cross is still the means to sift those who claim to be followers of Jesus. There are those of us who

Day 39

willingly take up the cross and follow him wherever he may lead, but some of us betray him in order to fit in to this world's systems. Others of us deny him for the comfort and praise of people. Still others despise the cross by fading into the background, not making a stand either for or against the cross.

Jesus gave us his kingdom (Luke 22:29). Will we stand for it or choose the kingdom of this world above it?

Prayer

Father, today we choose to fix our eyes on Jesus, the pioneer and perfecter of faith who, for the joy set before him, endured the cross, scorning its shame, and sat down at the right hand of the throne of God. Help us to consider him who endured such opposition from sinners so that we will not grow weary and lose heart. Amen. (Hebrews 12:2–3)

Meditation

1. Does the way you live your life affirm or deny the sacrifice of Jesus on the cross? How?

Remember

2. What is God challenging you to do today?

Day 40

Scripture Reading: Luke 22:39-46

Jesus went out as usual to the Mount of Olives, and his disciples followed him. (Luke 22:39)

Devotional Reflection

Jesus went out to the Mount of Olives to pray. This was apparently his usual routine.

This reminds me of Daniel, who was so predictable in his prayer life that it was easy to arrange for him to be thrown into the lion's den (Daniel 6). We need to be so predictable in our prayer lives that Satan can set his clock by us. This does not exclude spontaneous and consistent prayer, but the discipline of a time and a place of prayer are of great importance.

It is important because, without it, we cannot resist temptation. The disciples were too tired to pray. They were overtaken by sorrow, and prayer was too difficult for them. So, unlike Daniel, they yielded to every temptation that came their way on the way to Calvary.

Temptation is guaranteed to come; we should prepare for it long before it arrives. We prepare ourselves by having a disciplined prayer life. This way God will strengthen us (Luke 22:43), and we will overcome.

Burning Hearts

Prayer

Father, today we put on the full armor of God so we may be able to stand against the evil one. We pray in the Spirit on all occasions with all kinds of prayers and requests. With this in mind, help us to be alert and always praying for all the Lord's people. Amen. (Ephesians 6:11, 18)

Meditation

1. What are the areas in your life where you are sure to be tempted and where you generally submit to the temptation?

2. What is God challenging you to do today?

Day 41

Scripture Reading: Luke 22:47–53

But this is your hour—when darkness reigns. (Luke 22:53b)

Devotional Reflection

After praying for strength in the garden, Jesus and his disciples were confronted by the angry mob, led by Judas, who came to arrest Jesus. Everything happened just as Jesus predicted. Judas betrayed him, and Peter denied him.

Judas tried to pretend by kissing Jesus, but Jesus knew exactly what he was up to. Peter followed at a distance, but Jesus knew his location all the time. This hour of darkness was a time when Satan was given the opportunity to have free reign, but God was still in control of everything.

This hour of darkness reached further than just a dispute between Jesus and the religious leaders; it was an epic battle between the forces of darkness and those of light. Darkness was reigning, but it was only for a little while. Light would reign forever after this.

We all go through times when we feel we are caught in an hour of darkness. An hour when it feels as if Satan reigns. However, keep these things in mind: It is only for an hour. Weeping may last for a night, but

Joy and Amazement

joy comes in the morning. God is still in control even if it does not seem like it. He is aware of everything that is happening and will work it out for the best for those who trust him. Finally, remember that light always wins.

Prayer

Father, I know you are the light of the world and that whoever follows you will never walk in darkness but will have the light of life. Help me to believe this in my hour of darkness. Amen. (John 8:12)

Meditation

1. Think about a time when you felt that you were going through an hour of darkness. How did God bring his light into the situation?

2. What is God challenging you to do today?

Day 42

A Cause for Great Joy

Scripture Reading: Luke 23:1–25

From what he had heard about him, he hoped to see him perform a sign of some sort. (Luke 23:8b)

Devotional Reflection

Herod found himself in the midst of the biggest, most conclusive sign that God would ever give to humankind, but he was too blind to see it. He was privileged to have an encounter with John the Baptist, who could have prepared him for this moment. Instead he beheaded John. Now he was face to face with the Son of God, yet his eyes were veiled.

The crowds also missed it. They had front-row seats to all the miracles of Jesus. They had the honor of listening to his teachings and even his prophecies; yet they were totally oblivious to the mighty act of salvation taking place right under their noses.

Pilate had the slightest inclination of the injustice taking place. He found no fault with Jesus. However, he chose to wash his hands to demonstrate that he was innocent of the blood of Jesus (Matthew 27:24).

The only sign God gives is that of the cross. We can stop looking to the world for it. God revealed this great mystery to us by his grace (Matthew 11:25). We all face many circumstances that leave

❧ Prayer Requests and Praises

us doubting and questioning and looking for a sign from God. God has already responded because all of his promises are yes and amen in Christ Jesus (2 Corinthians 1:20).

Prayer

Father, we thank you because we know that it does not matter how many promises you have made; they are yes in Christ. And so through him we can say "Amen" to the glory of God. Amen.

Meditation

1. In which way is the cross God's answer to the current challenges you face?

2. What is God challenging you to do today?

Scripture Reading: Luke 23:26–43

Jesus turned and said to them, "Daughters of Jerusalem, do not weep for me; weep for yourselves and for your children." (Luke 23:28)

Devotional Reflection

The cross was the expression of God's love and grace for all human beings. It was a demonstration of the great lengths he would go to ensure the salvation of everyone because he is not willing that anyone should die in their sins (2 Peter 3:9).

There is, however, a warning in all of this to those who reject the love of God that is revealed in the sacrifice of his one and only Son. Jesus warned of a terrible time when God's justice will be revealed and people would wish that the mountains would fall on them so they could escape the wrath of God.

Two criminals were crucified with Jesus. One mocked him, and the other begged him for mercy. One made it into paradise, but the other would have to face the judgment of God. This judgment is coming (Revelation 20:11–15); we have to make sure we have accepted Jesus Christ and have lived to glorify him in our lives.

Prayer

Father, we know that judgment will begin with your household and that it will begin with us. This is why we commit ourselves to you, our faithful Creator, and will continue to do good. Amen. (1 Peter 4:17–19)

Meditation

1. What are your beliefs concerning God's judgment? Are they scriptural?

2. What is God challenging you to do today?

Scripture Reading: Luke 23:44–56

Jesus called out with a loud voice, "Father, into your hands I commit my spirit." When he had said this, he breathed his last. (Luke 23:46)

Devotional Reflection

Jesus is the perfect example of what it means to surrender everything to God. The account in Luke emphasizes his innocence. Even the Gentile centurion testified to his innocence, yet Jesus did not waver in his submission to God.

Jesus gave up his life, he entrusted his spirit to God, he held nothing back. His innocence and the injustice of the crucifixion did not cause any wavering in him. He drank the last drop from his bitter cup.

Even his burial testified to his innocence. Normally criminals would all just be thrown into one pit after their execution, but Jesus was buried in a new tomb. This emphasized not only his innocence but also his kingly office. The response of the crowds also revealed his innocence. They beat on their chests and wailed. This signified their remorse at all that had happened.

In all of this, Jesus did not waver in his reverent submission to God. His submission was complete, even unto death. We must follow the example of Jesus. If

Resist a Little Longer

we profess to be crucified with Christ, we too must entrust our spirits to God. We must hold nothing back, even if it appears as if we are being persecuted unfairly.

Our reverent submission will serve as a testimony not only of our innocence but also of the love and grace of God. It will serve to make people aware of their lost state and of the open curtain of grace that is available to all who will believe.

Prayer

Father, into your hands we commit our spirits. Amen.

Meditation

1. Name the areas in your life where you still need to reverently submit to God.

2. What is God challenging you to do today?

Day 1

Resist a Little Longer

Scripture Reading: Luke 24:1–12

Then they remembered his words. (Luke 24:8)

Devotional Reflection

The disciples had a short memory. Jesus prophesied about his death and resurrection on various occasions and in various ways. He tried to prepare them for all that was about to happen, but they could not perceive it.

In the resurrection account, the women went to go and embalm the body only to find that it was gone and that there were angels there instead. The angels asked them if they remembered that Jesus told them he would die and rise again. This triggered their memory. Then they remembered what Jesus had said.

The rest of the disciples were also incredulous, even though Jesus spoke to them on several occasions about these things. Peter had to run to the grave himself to make sure the women were telling the truth. They also needed to be reminded of all Jesus had said.

It is only human to forget, especially when one is faced with difficulty, trauma, or trials. However, God is so gracious that he makes sure to remind us of all the things he has taught us on our journey of

ॐ Day 1

faith. The most important truth we must remember when faced with trouble is that Christ rose from the dead. He defeated death and sin and hell. He overcame the power of the enemy and gained eternal victory for us. This is why we can overcome any situation—because Jesus overcame *for* us.

Prayer

Father, we praise you because in your great mercy you have given us new birth into the living hope through the resurrection of Jesus Christ from the dead, and into an inheritance that can never perish, spoil, or fade. Amen. (1 Peter 1:3–4)

Meditation

1. What great truths is the Holy Spirit reminding you of today?

2. What is God challenging you to do today?

Resist a Little Longer

✺ Day 1

Scripture Reading: Luke 24:13–35

They asked each other, "Were not our hearts burning within us while he talked with us on the road and opened the Scriptures to us?" (Luke 24:32)

Devotional Reflection

The two disciples on the road to Emmaus had a life-changing experience. They were in the presence of Jesus, the Son of God. This happened at a very low point in their lives, a time of disappointment and hopelessness.

They had put their hope and trust in Jesus, following him and hoping he was the Messiah, the one who would redeem Israel. But then he got killed, and, even worse, it seemed as if his body had been stolen. Everything seemed hopeless.

However, the hopelessness would not last long. They met Jesus on their way home. He explained the Scriptures to them, and their hearts burned in his presence. They did not recognize him, but they did not accept being separated from him, so they asked him to spend the night. As he broke the bread their eyes were opened, and they saw him, Jesus.

Our hearts can recognize the Savior, even when our heads don't. This burning of the heart is our response to the invitation of love. It is our leaning in

Resist a Little Longer

toward him, even when we don't fully understand our own reaction. It is what spurs us into action. Just like these disciples, we are ready to run back to Jerusalem in the evening to proclaim the good news that Jesus is risen.

Prayer

Father, may your grace be poured out on us abundantly, along with the faith and love that are in Christ Jesus. Amen. (1 Timothy 1:14)

Meditation

1. Can you recall occasions when your heart was burning in the presence of Jesus?

2. What is God challenging you to do today?

ಇ Day 1

Scripture Reading: Luke 24:36–49

And . . . they still did not believe it because of joy and amazement . . . (Luke 24:41)

Devotional Reflection

Can joy and amazement result in unbelief? It can when you want something so much that the possibility of it gives you joy and amazement, yet you find yourself too afraid to believe it, just in case it is not real. It might be that you think you will not recover if you should be disappointed again.

The reality of the resurrection of Jesus Christ from the dead *is* real. He is everything he professed to be, and he did all he predicted he would do. And he is doing all that he promised he would do at this very minute. That is why we can allow the joy and amazement to take its full course. We serve a risen Savior!

He is risen, but that's not all! We can also expect "power from on high" (Luke 24:49), the blessed Holy Spirit, who is in us and with us. That is the presence of the living God inside of us, giving us the means to live out this joy and amazement every day. Praise God!

Resist a Little Longer

Prayer

Jesus, we know you love us just as much as the Father loves you. Help us to remain in your love so our joy may be complete. Amen. (John 15:11)

Meditation

1. In what ways does the joy of your salvation manifest in your life?

2. What is God challenging you to do today?

ꙮ Day 1

Scripture Reading: Luke 24:50–53

Then they worshiped him and returned to Jerusalem with great joy. (Luke 24:52)

Devotional Reflection

Jesus was just given back to them. He was alive, and he met with them and taught them again, and now he was leaving again. He went up to heaven right before their eyes.

Why was this a cause of great joy? What does the ascension of Jesus mean to us? To the disciples, it meant that the gift of the Holy Spirit, the promised power from on high, would come down on them. Maybe they remembered the words of Jesus: "And I will ask the Father, and he will give you another advocate to help you and be with you forever—the Spirit of truth" (John 14:16–17a).

The ascension of Jesus into heaven led to the descent of the Holy Spirit on his disciples. Furthermore, Jesus is now continuing his ministry to us as he sits at the right hand of the Father, interceding for us (Romans 8:34).

We did not lose Jesus when he returned to heaven; we were just enabled to receive him in all his fullness. This is the cause of great joy—Christ in us, the hope of glory.

Resist a Little Longer

Prayer

Father, please fill us with all joy and peace as we trust in you so that we may overflow with hope by the power of the Holy Spirit. Amen. (Romans 15:13)

Meditation

1. What does the ascension mean to you?

2. What is God challenging you to do today?

Day 1

Resist a Little Longer

Day 1

Resist a Little Longer

Day 1

Resist a Little Longer

Day 1